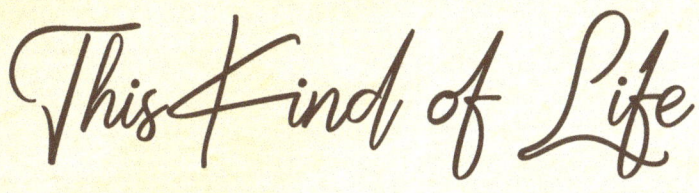

This Kind of Life

Healing & Grief Journal

This Journal helps express the many different feelings &
emotions that are often felt after a loss…

Brittaney A. Kersey

COPYRIGHT *Page*

This Kind of Life: A Healing & Grief Journal

First Printing
ISBN# ISBN: 978-1-955148-50-4 pbk

A2Z Books Publishing Lithonia, GA 30058
www.A2ZBooksPublishing.net Manufactured in the United States of America A2Z Books Publishing has allowed this work to remain exactly as the author intended, verbatim.

This Journal

BELONGS TO

_____

_____

_____

CONTENTS

INTRODUCTION

I am so honored this journal has reached you. This journal has been a long time coming; created out of a stagnant emotional time when I found it hard to find the joy and excitement in life. I've read many books and written in many journals without realizing what I was doing was navigating through grief and finding my way to healing.

Trying to find my way through life after a loss was difficult, especially with the wave of emotions that affected not only my life but also the lives of the people I love. After the loss of my mother, nothing in life has felt the same. Waking up and getting out of bed each day was hard. Holidays were dreaded, the change of seasons felt dull, and the air outside felt stale and didn't even smell the same. There was no joy in anything I did, big or small. How could I go on in this life when I was missing the very person who brought me here? She was not only my mother, but my best friend, my confidant, and as cliche as it sounds, my other half. I felt guilty going on with my life without her. I felt guilty for laughing at someone's funny joke or going out with friends, I even removed myself from social media for two years. Why would I want to laugh or engage with other people when a part of me has died? There was nothing funny or entertaining to me at the time, at all…

I did not realize that the emotions I felt were a part of the grieving journey. I worked out, fasted, dieted, read books, wrote in my notebook, and did what felt natural to me. I searched for a journal that specifically pointed out the many different emotions that I personally felt. Without finding it, I created it for myself with This Kind Of Life.

When I was younger, I couldn't imagine living "This Kind Of Life". The kind of life where I wouldn't have any parents, the kind of life where I would fall in and out of depression, the kind of life where my anxiety would leave me in isolation mode, the kind of life that would allow my emotions to take control and leave me feeling stuck. Often, we don't realize the thoughts, feelings, and emotions we experience while grieving are normal. So, I made sure to list every feeling I felt during this journey in hopes it can help you on your journey to healing after a loss.

Tracking my feelings with This Kind Of Life and noticing how it gave me an understanding which then gave me peace was one of the biggest positive changes I saw within myself after writing day to day. I hope if anything, This Kind Of Life serves as a tool for you to heal and take back control of your life after loss. Remember, grief comes in waves, and it is your JOURNEY.
I stand behind the mission of taking back control of your life and not allowing yourself to stay down, I pray you feel the urge to do so when using This Kind Of Life.

With Gratitude,

Brittaney

DEDICATION

To my mother,
my best friend, my other half, the pain of having to live a life without you is indescribable. I owe it to you to continue living the life you birthed me to live. Mommy, you were one of a kind, and your infectious smile, personality, and spirit will never be forgotten.

To my father,
I wish we had more time and memories. You will never be forgotten.

To my soulful Aunt Trudy,
Thank You for always reminding me of the strong, intelligent woman I am. I will forever be your "Sistah Souljah." We miss you so much.

To Grandma Trish & Aunt Brooke,
It is because of your strength and guidance that we have made it this far. Life has never been perfect, but as a family, we do our best.
Thank you for everything.

To my siblings,
You are stronger than you know, and I will always be here to remind you of the strength Mommy instilled in each of us.

To Kareem,
Thank you for holding me down during my darkest days.

Mom, Dad, Aunt Trudy, Aunt Marian, Aunt Bobby, Uncle Ronnie, Uncle William, & Mike Reynolds May your souls rest in eternal peace.

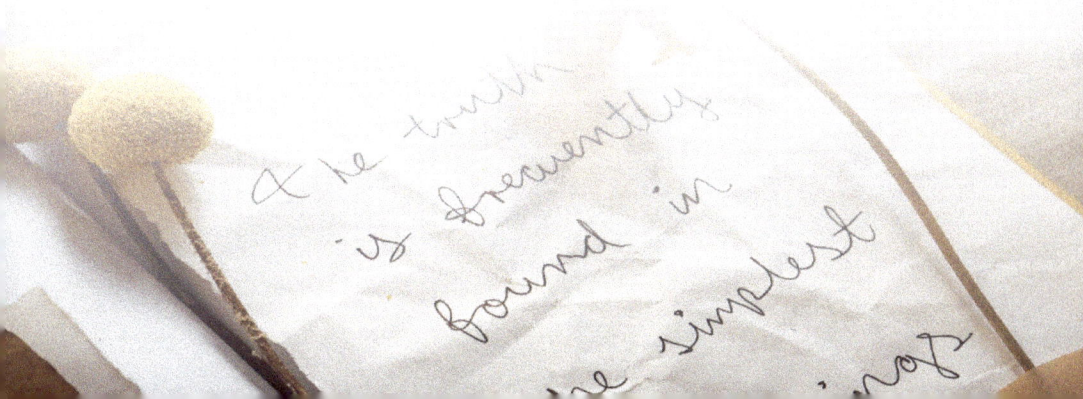

COMMITMENT

I _____ am making the decision to intentionally process my thoughts, feelings, & emotions as I navigate my way through grief. I understand that what I feel is normal and it's ok to not be ok. I will not allow my pain or my intruding thoughts to take control of my life. I will give myself grace and the time I deserve to allow myself to feel so that I can heal. I will give myself the space to rest, to reflect, and to shed the layers of my previous self. I understand that there is no returning to the "old me" because there will be an evolved me and a new normal that I must get to know. I understand that this journey will take time and will not happen overnight. I understand that I may grow in cycles and heal in seasons. I will fight to get up each day and find the joy in life again. I will take care of myself starting with my mind and body. I understand that I only get one life and one body, and I must be intentional with both. I will not give up on myself or my life. I deserve peace. I deserve healing. I deserve to take back control of my life.

I make this commitment to myself from this day forward.

Signature _____   Date _____

LETTER TO *Myself*

Think about where you want to be one year from now mentally, physically, & emotionally and write a letter to that person.

Dear _____

_____

_____

_____

_____

_____

_____

_____

_____

_____

_____

_____

_____

_____

_____

_____

_____

_____

_____

_____

_____

_____

_____

_____

_____

WHAT IS  ?

Grieving is a normal and healthy response to pain and loss and an essential process to help cope. However, grief is one of the most difficult human emotions because it has many different layers and effects.

When we hear the word grief, we often think of when someone passes away. Although I believe the grief that is experienced after someone transitions from this life is the highest form of grief, someone doesn't have to necessarily die for a person to experience grief.

As humans, we can grieve any significant loss. The loss of a relationship, marriage, friendship, and even the loss of a job or career can leave us in a state of grief.

At some point in each of our lives, we will experience grief—often, more than once. There are different stages in grief and each stage may manifest itself in different ways and may often come in "waves". Each grief experience is unique to the person. We have our own perspective and feelings that impact the grieving journey, I say "journey" because that's exactly what it is, it is not a process but more of a journey. A process is something you get through, but a journey is something you go through and the grieving journey has no expiration.

One of my favorite quotes is "Death is not the greatest loss in life, the greatest loss is what dies inside while still alive". I love this quote because it reminds us that the biggest loss is when we lose ourselves. Whatever and whoever we are grieving would want us to continue to live and take back control of our lives. You deserve to be happy, you deserve to live the life you would have lived before your loss, you deserve to have peace, you deserve to live the kind of life that makes you feel free! Free of heartache, free of depression, free of guilt!

I am grieving the loss of _____

AFFIRMATION

I know sadness is normal and I will allow myself to feel and be in this moment. Tomorrow I will do something that will bring me happiness and make me smile even if that something is small.

WORD Search

```
F M X E Y J Y S H D P U N X O Z Z T B V W E U
S C T S I T A H S F M E H E A B N U L L I A C
A O B R K Z A H J G P O P I V V A O P H Y C Y
P S A O E H D S Q H U L E C E X K Z G E R A O
Y Y R M H B L Q K P C I C R K I W G H T U C D
O D G E W I E D I C Y R L B X H X Z S T M R D
J V A R R Q F E I R G T H T E X O U S E Y S S
S I I S R E K H I N J N I Q K N N U E R F L E
R N N R W J L Z D L A I N E D Q A M N G A U F
S R I O J J J E T Q E I S X G M N K B E X D D
K Z N V T H E W A Q D T S X S A G C M R F M N
C L G I C C O A Q S Q F E X G U E L U N Y X P
G K M V D E J F A G E B N B Y K R P N J B U L
U F M R C A M I V W G M D W T B X M Q C R H H
F P T U F N L N E R X K A R R T P H G S J C B
Z O W S O U S D C K X J S P R A T Y R C O Z M
```

Find the following words in the puzzle.
Words are hidden ↑ ↓ → ← and ↘.

ANGER   GUILT   SADNESS
BARGAINING   NUMBNESS   SURVIVORS REMORSE
DENIAL   REGRET
GRIEF   RELEASE

Date: _____

Time:_____

MOOD

What I'm feeling today:

_____

What I'm most hopeful for today:

_____

_____

_____

My most triggering thought today:

_____

_____

_____

My most inspiring thought today:

_____

_____

_____

My focus tomorrow will be:

_____

_____

_____

SELF CARE *Checklist*

In the state of grief, it can be difficult to complete our basic day to day tasks and routine. Taking care of our hygiene and nourishing our bodies is important to our wellbeing. This chart is a tool to help stay on track of our personal hygiene and self care.

- ○ Wake Up
- ○ Make my bed
- ○ Shower
- ○ Wash my face
- ○ Brush my teeth
- ○ Comb/Brush my hair
- ○ Change into fresh Clothes
- ○ Moisturize

- ○ Drink water
- ○ Take Vitamins
- ○ Eat Fruit
- ○ Journal
- ○ Read
- ○ Workout
- ○ Go on a Nature Walk
- ○ Recite Affirmation

Be Patient with yourself and do what you can...

I take comfort in the positive memories.

_____

_____

_____

GRIEF JOURNALING *Page*

Journaling is a way to release what's inside of you and express how you feel.

Freely Express yourself here……

_____

_____

_____

_____

_____

_____

_____

_____

_____

_____

_____

_____

_____

_____

_____

_____

_____

_____

_____

_____

GRIEF JOURNALING *Page*

Journaling is a way to release what's inside of you and express how you feel.

Freely Express yourself here......

_____

_____

_____

_____

_____

_____

_____

_____

_____

_____

_____

_____

_____

_____

_____

_____

_____

_____

_____

_____

_____

Date: _____

Time:_____

EMOTION *Tracker*

What I'm feeling today:

_____

What I'm most hopeful for today:

_____
_____
_____

My most triggering thought today:

_____
_____
_____

My most inspiring thought today:

_____
_____
_____

My focus tomorrow will be:

_____
_____
_____

Date: _____

Time:_____

EMOTION *Tracker*

What I'm feeling today:

_____

What I'm most hopeful for today:

_____

_____

_____

My most triggering thought today:

_____

_____

_____

My most inspiring thought today:

_____

_____

_____

My focus tomorrow will be:

_____

_____

_____

SELF CARE *Checklist*

In the state of grief, it can be difficult to complete our basic day to day tasks and routine. Taking care of our hygiene and nourishing our bodies is important to our wellbeing. This chart is a tool to help stay on track of our personal hygiene and self care.

- ○ Wake Up
- ○ Make my bed
- ○ Shower
- ○ Wash my face
- ○ Brush my teeth
- ○ Comb/Brush my hair
- ○ Change into fresh Clothes
- ○ Moisturize

- ○ Drink water
- ○ Take Vitamins
- ○ Eat Fruit
- ○ Journal
- ○ Read
- ○ Workout
- ○ Go on a Nature Walk
- ○ Recite Affirmation

Be Patient with yourself and do what you can...

I choose to feel the presence of my grief.

_____

_____

_____

GRIEF JOURNALING *Page*

Journaling is a way to release what's inside of you and express how you feel.

Freely Express yourself here......

_____

_____

_____

_____

_____

_____

_____

_____

_____

_____

_____

_____

_____

_____

_____

_____

_____

_____

_____

_____

GRIEF JOURNALING *Page*

Journaling is a way to release what's inside of you and express how you feel.

Freely Express yourself here……

_____

_____

_____

_____

_____

_____

_____

_____

_____

_____

_____

_____

_____

_____

_____

_____

_____

_____

_____

_____

_____

_____

Date: _____

Time:_____

EMOTION *Tracker*

What I'm feeling today:

_____

What I'm most hopeful for today:

_____
_____
_____

My most triggering thought today:

_____
_____
_____

My most inspiring thought today:

_____
_____
_____

My focus tomorrow will be:

_____
_____
_____

Date: _____

Time: _____

EMOTION  *Tracker*

What I'm feeling today:

_____

What I'm most hopeful for today:

_____

_____

_____

My most triggering thought today:

_____

_____

_____

My most inspiring thought today:

_____

_____

_____

My focus tomorrow will be:

_____

_____

_____

SELF CARE *Checklist*

In the state of grief, it can be difficult to complete our basic day to day tasks and routine. Taking care of our hygiene and nourishing our bodies is important to our wellbeing. This chart is a tool to help stay on track of our personal hygiene and self care.

- ◯ Wake Up
- ◯ Make my bed
- ◯ Shower
- ◯ Wash my face
- ◯ Brush my teeth
- ◯ Comb/Brush my hair
- ◯ Change into fresh Clothes
- ◯ Moisturize

- ◯ Drink water
- ◯ Take Vitamins
- ◯ Eat Fruit
- ◯ Journal
- ◯ Read
- ◯ Workout
- ◯ Go on a Nature Walk
- ◯ Recite Affirmation

Be Patient with yourself and do what you can...

WRITE & RECITE *Affirmation*

I give myself time and space to feel all my feelings.

_____

_____

_____

GRIEF JOURNALING *Page*

Journaling is a way to release what's inside of you and express how you feel.

Freely Express yourself here……

_____

_____

_____

_____

_____

_____

_____

_____

_____

_____

_____

_____

_____

_____

_____

_____

_____

_____

_____

_____

GRIEF JOURNALING *Page*

Journaling is a way to release what's inside of you and express how you feel.

Freely Express yourself here......

_____

_____

_____

_____

_____

_____

_____

_____

_____

_____

_____

_____

_____

_____

_____

_____

_____

_____

_____

EMOTION *Tracker*

What I'm feeling today:

_____

What I'm most hopeful for today:

_____
_____
_____

My most triggering thought today:

_____
_____
_____

My most inspiring thought today:

_____
_____
_____

My focus tomorrow will be:

_____
_____
_____

AFFIRMATION

It's ok that I need time to grieve.

WORD *Search*

```
P  S  H  B  N  K  N  R  E  L  E  A  S  E  N  Z  E  I  W  Z  N  P  S
A  H  S  S  E  N  S  S  E  L  P  L  E  H  S  J  P  C  S  M  T  A  S
F  W  Y  T  N  U  B  Z  T  V  N  I  W  O  M  V  T  L  D  Q  C  A  V
H  F  Q  B  Q  A  N  X  I  E  T  Y  N  B  N  X  Y  M  J  A  S  U  K
S  D  Q  Q  N  U  C  V  P  V  D  G  P  X  E  H  U  B  B  P  L  Q  W
S  K  X  N  O  I  T  A  L  O  S  I  G  G  W  W  L  G  Y  F  J  S  G
E  Q  G  I  P  L  Z  Q  T  S  S  E  N  L  U  F  T  E  G  R  O  F  E
N  Q  D  F  R  C  S  E  J  B  M  H  P  C  D  N  V  R  X  E  M  O  E
I  S  C  U  V  P  D  E  A  T  H  V  N  I  E  C  I  N  A  P  D  W  S
L  K  O  Q  E  X  K  C  A  C  A  S  D  I  Q  Q  K  O  R  E  Q  K  P
E  Q  Q  F  A  W  Q  O  P  U  F  A  M  E  M  V  R  U  P  S  Z  S  U
N  V  C  E  X  W  F  T  H  P  K  H  R  R  Q  F  G  C  U  T  K  O  G
O  M  L  A  B  G  D  K  M  K  X  U  F  P  X  L  L  J  C  K  T  M  T
L  Z  G  R  Y  R  O  Z  O  Y  L  W  I  X  Q  C  M  L  R  E  F  R  Q
C  K  D  E  P  E  R  S  O  N  A  L  I  Z  A  T  I  O  N  I  N  T  L
N  Q  B  G  D  M  I  H  Z  V  G  L  T  S  X  F  R  M  Z  N  Z  Q  K
```

Find the following words in the puzzle.
Words are hidden ↑ ↓ → ← and ↘.

ANXIETY	FORGETFULNESS	PANIC
DEATH	HELPLESSNESS	RELEASE
DEPERSONALIZATION	ISOLATION	
FEAR	LONELINESS	

Date: _____

Time:_____

MOOD

What I'm feeling today:

_____

What I'm most hopeful for today:

_____

_____

_____

My most triggering thought today:

_____

_____

_____

My most inspiring thought today:

_____

_____

_____

My focus tomorrow will be:

_____

_____

_____

SELF CARE *Checklist*

In the state of grief, it can be difficult to complete our basic day to day tasks and routine. Taking care of our hygiene and nourishing our bodies is important to our wellbeing. This chart is a tool to help stay on track of our personal hygiene and self care.

- ○ Wake Up
- ○ Make my bed
- ○ Shower
- ○ Wash my face
- ○ Brush my teeth
- ○ Comb/Brush my hair
- ○ Change into fresh Clothes
- ○ Moisturize

- ○ Drink water
- ○ Take Vitamins
- ○ Eat Fruit
- ○ Journal
- ○ Read
- ○ Workout
- ○ Go on a Nature Walk
- ○ Recite Affirmation

Be Patient with yourself and do what you can...

WRITE & RECITE *Affirmation*

I can be gentle with myself as I heal.

_____

_____

_____

GRIEF JOURNALING *Page*

Journaling is a way to release what's inside of you and express how you feel.

Freely Express yourself here……

_____

_____

_____

_____

_____

_____

_____

_____

_____

_____

_____

_____

_____

_____

_____

_____

_____

_____

_____

GRIEF JOURNALING *Page*

Journaling is a way to release what's inside of you and express how you feel.

Freely Express yourself here……

_____

_____

_____

_____

_____

_____

_____

_____

_____

_____

_____

_____

_____

_____

_____

_____

_____

_____

_____

_____

EMOTION *Tracker*

What I'm feeling today:

_____

What I'm most hopeful for today:

_____

_____

_____

My most triggering thought today:

_____

_____

_____

My most inspiring thought today:

_____

_____

_____

My focus tomorrow will be:

_____

_____

_____

Date: _____

Time:_____

EMOTION

What I'm feeling today:

_____

What I'm most hopeful for today:

_____
_____
_____

My most triggering thought today:

_____
_____
_____

My most inspiring thought today:

_____
_____
_____

My focus tomorrow will be:

_____
_____
_____

SELF CARE *Checklist*

In the state of grief, it can be difficult to complete our basic day to day tasks and routine. Taking care of our hygiene and nourishing our bodies is important to our wellbeing. This chart is a tool to help stay on track of our personal hygiene and self care.

- Wake Up
- Make my bed
- Shower
- Wash my face
- Brush my teeth
- Comb/Brush my hair
- Change into fresh Clothes
- Moisturize

- Drink water
- Take Vitamins
- Eat Fruit
- Journal
- Read
- Workout
- Go on a Nature Walk
- Recite Affirmation

Be Patient with yourself and do what you can...

WRITE & RECITE *Affirmation*

I can ask for help if I need it.

_____

_____

_____

GRIEF JOURNALING *Page*

Journaling is a way to release what's inside of you and express how you feel.

Freely Express yourself here……

_____

_____

_____

_____

_____

_____

_____

_____

_____

_____

_____

_____

_____

_____

_____

_____

_____

_____

_____

_____

_____

GRIEF JOURNALING *Page*

Journaling is a way to release what's inside of you and express how you feel.

Freely Express yourself here……

_____

_____

_____

_____

_____

_____

_____

_____

_____

_____

_____

_____

_____

_____

_____

_____

_____

_____

_____

_____

_____

EMOTION *Tracker*

What I'm feeling today:

_____

What I'm most hopeful for today:

_____
_____
_____

My most triggering thought today:

_____
_____
_____

My most inspiring thought today:

_____
_____
_____

My focus tomorrow will be:

_____
_____
_____

Date: _____

Time: _____

EMOTION *Tracker*

What I'm feeling today:

_____

What I'm most hopeful for today:

_____

_____

_____

My most triggering thought today:

_____

_____

_____

My most inspiring thought today:

_____

_____

_____

My focus tomorrow will be:

_____

_____

_____

SELF CARE *Checklist*

In the state of grief, it can be difficult to complete our basic day to day tasks and routine. Taking care of our hygiene and nourishing our bodies is important to our wellbeing. This chart is a tool to help stay on track of our personal hygiene and self care.

- ○ Wake Up
- ○ Make my bed
- ○ Shower
- ○ Wash my face
- ○ Brush my teeth
- ○ Comb/Brush my hair
- ○ Change into fresh Clothes
- ○ Moisturize

- ○ Drink water
- ○ Take Vitamins
- ○ Eat Fruit
- ○ Journal
- ○ Read
- ○ Workout
- ○ Go on a Nature Walk
- ○ Recite Affirmation

Be Patient with yourself and do what you can...

WRITE & RECITE *Affirmation*

I am grateful for all the love in my life.

_____

_____

_____

GRIEF JOURNALING *Page*

Journaling is a way to release what's inside of you and express how you feel.

Freely Express yourself here......

_____

_____

_____

_____

_____

_____

_____

_____

_____

_____

_____

_____

_____

_____

_____

_____

_____

_____

_____

_____

_____

GRIEF JOURNALING *Page*

Journaling is a way to release what's inside of you and express how you feel.

Freely Express yourself here……

_____

_____

_____

_____

_____

_____

_____

_____

_____

_____

_____

_____

_____

_____

_____

_____

_____

_____

_____

_____

_____

Date: _____

Time:_____

EMOTION *Tracker*

What I'm feeling today:

_____

What I'm most hopeful for today:

_____

_____

_____

My most triggering thought today:

_____

_____

_____

My most inspiring thought today:

_____

_____

_____

My focus tomorrow will be:

_____

_____

_____

AFFIRMATION

I choose to feel at peace today.

WORD *Search*

```
A I W Q P O B S E R V A T I O N L H F H T F B
D Z B G D U G V C N N F X W M Z F M B W T T R
F X J D N U P C P E U C V D X R K Z U I Z B I
F X Y Q E Y B Y W F W N N O I T A Z I L A E R
F E T Y V G Y A W E K I N W J Q Q T I Y L P Z
Y X I C W R F M A S I T V H G D M D D V O T U
U H R Z D N O I T A N G A T S V K P G D T D U
T A E O X L U R K F V C O N F U S I O N G D S
C U P N G F Q N O I T A Z I N A G R O S I D J
E S S Y G R W L G M Q P H D I V F Z Q S G L U
L T O C F U F L G K T H G A D S I Y Y D U Y I
F I R L F K F Z C Q A G G Z X J N Y N O F Z C
E O P M O F G L R L S S E N I P P A H N O V C
R N X K A I D U X E N V Y J Z Z Q D H P N I L
E T X C C F L N Y H Z H G K O Y F X K A Z L X
R T H G K R Q Z W F M M U E Z T F T I B T Q U
```

Find the following words in the puzzle.
Words are hidden ↑ ↓ → ← and ↘.

CONFUSION

DISORGANIZATION

ENVY

EXHAUSTION

HAPPINESS

OBSERVATION

PROSPERITY

REALIZATION

REFLECT

STAGNATION

Date: _____

Time:_____

What I'm feeling today:

_____

What I'm most hopeful for today:

_____

_____

_____

My most triggering thought today:

_____

_____

_____

My most inspiring thought today:

_____

_____

_____

My focus tomorrow will be:

_____

_____

_____

SELF CARE *Checklist*

In the state of grief, it can be difficult to complete our basic day to day tasks and routine. Taking care of our hygiene and nourishing our bodies is important to our wellbeing. This chart is a tool to help stay on track of our personal hygiene and self care.

- ○ Wake Up
- ○ Make my bed
- ○ Shower
- ○ Wash my face
- ○ Brush my teeth
- ○ Comb/Brush my hair
- ○ Change into fresh Clothes
- ○ Moisturize

- ○ Drink water
- ○ Take Vitamins
- ○ Eat Fruit
- ○ Journal
- ○ Read
- ○ Workout
- ○ Go on a Nature Walk
- ○ Recite Affirmation

Be Patient with yourself and do what you can...

I can endure and survive this loss.

_____

_____

_____

GRIEF JOURNALING *Page*

Journaling is a way to release what's inside of you and express how you feel.

Freely Express yourself here......

_____

_____

_____

_____

_____

_____

_____

_____

_____

_____

_____

_____

_____

_____

_____

_____

_____

_____

_____

GRIEF JOURNALING *Page*

Journaling is a way to release what's inside of you and express how you feel.

Freely Express yourself here......

_____

_____

_____

_____

_____

_____

_____

_____

_____

_____

_____

_____

_____

_____

_____

_____

_____

_____

_____

_____

_____

_____

Date: _____

Time: _____

EMOTION *Tracker*

What I'm feeling today:

_____

What I'm most hopeful for today:

_____

_____

_____

My most triggering thought today:

_____

_____

_____

My most inspiring thought today:

_____

_____

_____

My focus tomorrow will be:

_____

_____

_____

Date: _____

Time: _____

EMOTION  *Tracker*

What I'm feeling today:

_____

What I'm most hopeful for today:

_____

_____

_____

My most triggering thought today:

_____

_____

_____

My most inspiring thought today:

_____

_____

_____

My focus tomorrow will be:

_____

_____

_____

SELF CARE *Checklist*

In the state of grief, it can be difficult to complete our basic day to day tasks and routine. Taking care of our hygiene and nourishing our bodies is important to our wellbeing. This chart is a tool to help stay on track of our personal hygiene and self care.

- ○ Wake Up
- ○ Make my bed
- ○ Shower
- ○ Wash my face
- ○ Brush my teeth
- ○ Comb/Brush my hair
- ○ Change into fresh Clothes
- ○ Moisturize

- ○ Drink water
- ○ Take Vitamins
- ○ Eat Fruit
- ○ Journal
- ○ Read
- ○ Workout
- ○ Go on a Nature Walk
- ○ Recite Affirmation

Be Patient with yourself and do what you can...

WRITE & RECITE *Affirmation*

Every one of my feelings is important.

_____

_____

_____

GRIEF JOURNALING *Page*

Journaling is a way to release what's inside of you and express how you feel.

Freely Express yourself here……

_____

_____

_____

_____

_____

_____

_____

_____

_____

_____

_____

_____

_____

_____

_____

_____

_____

_____

_____

_____

_____

GRIEF JOURNALING *Page*

Journaling is a way to release what's inside of you and express how you feel.

Freely Express yourself here……

_____

_____

_____

_____

_____

_____

_____

_____

_____

_____

_____

_____

_____

_____

_____

_____

_____

_____

_____

_____

_____

_____

Date: _____

Time: _____

EMOTION *Tracker*

What I'm feeling today:

_____

What I'm most hopeful for today:

_____

_____

_____

My most triggering thought today:

_____

_____

_____

My most inspiring thought today:

_____

_____

_____

My focus tomorrow will be:

_____

_____

_____

Date: _____

Time:_____

EMOTION

What I'm feeling today:

_____

What I'm most hopeful for today:

_____

_____

_____

My most triggering thought today:

_____

_____

_____

My most inspiring thought today:

_____

_____

_____

My focus tomorrow will be:

_____

_____

_____

SELF CARE *Checklist*

In the state of grief, it can be difficult to complete our basic day to day tasks and routine. Taking care of our hygiene and nourishing our bodies is important to our wellbeing. This chart is a tool to help stay on track of our personal hygiene and self care.

- ◯ Wake Up
- ◯ Make my bed
- ◯ Shower
- ◯ Wash my face
- ◯ Brush my teeth
- ◯ Comb/Brush my hair
- ◯ Change into fresh Clothes
- ◯ Moisturize

- ◯ Drink water
- ◯ Take Vitamins
- ◯ Eat Fruit
- ◯ Journal
- ◯ Read
- ◯ Workout
- ◯ Go on a Nature Walk
- ◯ Recite Affirmation

Be Patient with yourself and do what you can...

I am thankful for what I had and for what I still have.

_____

_____

_____

GRIEF JOURNALING *Page*

Journaling is a way to release what's inside of you and express how you feel.

Freely Express yourself here......

_____

_____

_____

_____

_____

_____

_____

_____

_____

_____

_____

_____

_____

_____

_____

_____

_____

_____

_____

_____

_____

GRIEF JOURNALING *Page*

Journaling is a way to release what's inside of you and express how you feel.

Freely Express yourself here……

_____

_____

_____

_____

_____

_____

_____

_____

_____

_____

_____

_____

_____

_____

_____

_____

_____

_____

_____

_____

Date: _____

Time: _____

EMOTION *Tracker*

What I'm feeling today:

_____

What I'm most hopeful for today:

_____

_____

_____

My most triggering thought today:

_____

_____

_____

My most inspiring thought today:

_____

_____

_____

My focus tomorrow will be:

_____

_____

_____

AFFIRMATION

I grieve because I love,
and I am thankful I can love.

WORD *Search*

```
U A D G O Z K H P S S O L K H B E C P Q I S U
P M T E L I P Q R W W A K L G U W K D Z J Z V
R R E V C Y V G Z U J S C L S E R D C J P O V
O L Q I T H D C Z N N F Y C A C E G A R U O C
G A V R L U B M J X O D P M E L Z J D P P C V
R N B R M V I C T O R Y E B L P O Q F N U X N
E O O G R O W T H W N O T R W B T F K X G S H
S I I Z I G T R I U M P H C S P W A Q V Q D P
S T Z H X D R F N J P F W I W T E E N A Z U H
V N C T J C U C F E I L E R D S A A E C N G Q
E E Q N B O U N D A R I E S V X E N C T E G C
V T K E J O Q U J G R Y Y B X B G E D E H P S
O N J R U O H V R H E A L I N G J O L I M P T
L I Z Y W E O L I P S Y F G F C V G E R N K P
L A I T D Y F A R T O A G M F Y O S V P J G R
C S T R A N S I T I O N F X A J Y L P L J M P
```

Find the following words in the puzzle.
Words are hidden ↑ ↓ → ← and ↘.

ACCEPTANCE	LOSS	TRIUMPH
BOUNDARIES	LOVE	UNDERSTANDING
COURAGE	PEACE	VICTORY
GROWTH	PROGRESS	
HEALING	RELIEF	
INTENTIONAL	TRANSITION	

Date: _____

Time:_____

MOOD

What I'm feeling today:

_____

What I'm most hopeful for today:

_____

_____

_____

My most triggering thought today:

_____

_____

_____

My most inspiring thought today:

_____

_____

_____

My focus tomorrow will be:

_____

_____

_____

SELF CARE *Checklist*

In the state of grief, it can be difficult to complete our basic day to day tasks and routine. Taking care of our hygiene and nourishing our bodies is important to our wellbeing. This chart is a tool to help stay on track of our personal hygiene and self care.

- Wake Up
- Make my bed
- Shower
- Wash my face
- Brush my teeth
- Comb/Brush my hair
- Change into fresh Clothes
- Moisturize

- Drink water
- Take Vitamins
- Eat Fruit
- Journal
- Read
- Workout
- Go on a Nature Walk
- Recite Affirmation

Be Patient with yourself and do what you can...

WRITE & RECITE *Affirmation*

I will take as much time as I need to grieve this loss.

_____

_____

_____

GRIEF JOURNALING *Page*

Journaling is a way to release what's inside of you and express how you feel.

Freely Express yourself here……

_____

_____

_____

_____

_____

_____

_____

_____

_____

_____

_____

_____

_____

_____

_____

_____

_____

_____

_____

_____

_____

GRIEF JOURNALING *Page*

Journaling is a way to release what's inside of you and express how you feel.

Freely Express yourself here……

_____

_____

_____

_____

_____

_____

_____

_____

_____

_____

_____

_____

_____

_____

_____

_____

_____

_____

_____

_____

_____

_____

Date: _____

Time: _____

EMOTION

What I'm feeling today:

_____

What I'm most hopeful for today:

_____

_____

_____

My most triggering thought today:

_____

_____

_____

My most inspiring thought today:

_____

_____

_____

My focus tomorrow will be:

_____

_____

_____

Date: _____

Time: _____

EMOTION  *Tracker*

What I'm feeling today:

_____

What I'm most hopeful for today:

_____

_____

_____

My most triggering thought today:

_____

_____

_____

My most inspiring thought today:

_____

_____

_____

My focus tomorrow will be:

_____

_____

_____

SELF CARE *Checklist*

In the state of grief, it can be difficult to complete our basic day to day tasks and routine. Taking care of our hygiene and nourishing our bodies is important to our wellbeing. This chart is a tool to help stay on track of our personal hygiene and self care.

- ○ Wake Up
- ○ Make my bed
- ○ Shower
- ○ Wash my face
- ○ Brush my teeth
- ○ Comb/Brush my hair
- ○ Change into fresh Clothes
- ○ Moisturize

- ○ Drink water
- ○ Take Vitamins
- ○ Eat Fruit
- ○ Journal
- ○ Read
- ○ Workout
- ○ Go on a Nature Walk
- ○ Recite Affirmation

Be Patient with yourself and do what you can...

It is ok for me not to be strong right now.

_____

_____

_____

GRIEF JOURNALING *Page*

Journaling is a way to release what's inside of you and express how you feel.

Freely Express yourself here……

_____

_____

_____

_____

_____

_____

_____

_____

_____

_____

_____

_____

_____

_____

_____

_____

_____

_____

_____

_____

_____

GRIEF JOURNALING *Page*

Journaling is a way to release what's inside of you and express how you feel.

Freely Express yourself here……

_____

_____

_____

_____

_____

_____

_____

_____

_____

_____

_____

_____

_____

_____

_____

_____

_____

_____

_____

_____

_____

Date: _____

Time: _____

EMOTION *Tracker*

What I'm feeling today:

_____

What I'm most hopeful for today:

_____
_____
_____

My most triggering thought today:

_____
_____
_____

My most inspiring thought today:

_____
_____
_____

My focus tomorrow will be:

_____
_____
_____

Date: _____

Time: _____

EMOTION *Tracker*

What I'm feeling today:

_____

What I'm most hopeful for today:

_____

_____

_____

My most triggering thought today:

_____

_____

_____

My most inspiring thought today:

_____

_____

_____

My focus tomorrow will be:

_____

_____

_____

SELF CARE *Checklist*

In the state of grief, it can be difficult to complete our basic day to day tasks and routine. Taking care of our hygiene and nourishing our bodies is important to our wellbeing. This chart is a tool to help stay on track of our personal hygiene and self care.

- ○ Wake Up
- ○ Make my bed
- ○ Shower
- ○ Wash my face
- ○ Brush my teeth
- ○ Comb/Brush my hair
- ○ Change into fresh Clothes
- ○ Moisturize

- ○ Drink water
- ○ Take Vitamins
- ○ Eat Fruit
- ○ Journal
- ○ Read
- ○ Workout
- ○ Go on a Nature Walk
- ○ Recite Affirmation

Be Patient with yourself and do what you can...

WRITE & RECITE *Affirmation*

I accept that I will feel tired sometimes; I will rest when needed.

_____

_____

_____

GRIEF JOURNALING *Page*

Journaling is a way to release what's inside of you and express how you feel.

Freely Express yourself here......

_____

_____

_____

_____

_____

_____

_____

_____

_____

_____

_____

_____

_____

_____

_____

_____

_____

_____

_____

_____

_____

GRIEF JOURNALING *Page*

Journaling is a way to release what's inside of you and express how you feel.

Freely Express yourself here……

_____

_____

_____

_____

_____

_____

_____

_____

_____

_____

_____

_____

_____

_____

_____

_____

_____

_____

_____

_____

Date: _____

Time: _____

EMOTION  *Tracker*

What I'm feeling today:

_____

What I'm most hopeful for today:

_____
_____
_____

My most triggering thought today:

_____
_____
_____

My most inspiring thought today:

_____
_____
_____

My focus tomorrow will be:

_____
_____
_____

Date: _____

Time:_____

EMOTION *Tracker*

What I'm feeling today:

_____

What I'm most hopeful for today:

_____

_____

_____

My most triggering thought today:

_____

_____

_____

My most inspiring thought today:

_____

_____

_____

My focus tomorrow will be:

_____

_____

_____

Death is not the greatest loss in life.
The greatest loss
is what dies inside while still alive.
Never Surrender.

Tupac Shakur

ABOUT THE *Author*

Brittaney Kersey was born and raised in the Frankford section of Philadelphia, PA. on August 11, 1992. She was raised by three strong independent women, her mother, grandmother, and aunt. Each has played a major role in her upbringing and the woman she is today. After the passing of her mother in 2013, Brittaney did a lot of soul searching and inner work on herself. Trying to cope with the changes in her life, Brittaney started working out, reading, journaling, and taking care of her mind, body, and spirit. Because of this, wellness and personal development became one of her passions and she found purpose in encouraging others who are on the same journey. Driven by purpose and fueled by pain, Brittaney is an advocate of navigating life after loss and taking back control of your life starting with your mind and body. This journal is only the beginning of what she has to share and offer to the people out there who are walking the same path.

Contact Info: Email brittaney56241@gmail.com
Facebook: Brittaney Kersey
Instagram: @ambk__

Interested in Writing and or Publishing a Book?
Visit **a2zbookspublishing.net**

www.ingramcontent.com/pod-product-compliance
Lightning Source LLC
Chambersburg PA
CBHW051641120626
46551CB00014B/2163